STARTERS
PLACES

Israel

Macdonald Educational

About Starters Places

Starters Places provide an entertaining and informative introduction for young children to various countries and their national characteristics.

The vocabulary is controlled for reading by young children, and about 90 per cent of the words in the book should be familiar to young readers.

Each book contains material for further activities and research, such as an easy reference map, a table of simple facts, a project, a dictionary and an index.

Teachers and experts have been consulted on the content and accuracy of the books.

Illustrated by: William Hewison

Written and planned by: Sandie Oram

Managing editor: Su Swallow

Editorial assistant: Diana Darley

Production: Stephen Pawley, Rosemary Bishop

Art consultant: Geoffrey Dickinson of *Punch*

Reading consultant: Donald Moyle, author of *The Teaching of Reading* and senior lecturer in education at Edge Hill College of Education

Chairman, teacher advisory panel: F. F. Blackwell, Director, Primary Extension Programme, National Council for Educational Technology; general inspector for schools (primary), London Borough of Croydon

Teacher panel: Loveday Harmer, Lynda Snowdon, Joy West, Enid Wilkinson

Colour reproduction by Colourcraftsmen Limited

© Macdonald and Company (Publishers) Limited 1973
ISBN 0 356 04318 5
Made and printed in England by Hazell Watson & Viney Ltd Aylesbury, Buckinghamshire

Filmset by Layton-Sun Limited

First published 1973 by Macdonald and Company (Publishers) Limited
St. Giles House
49-50 Poland Street
London W1

bread

candlestick

Many Jewish people live in Israel.
Saturday is their Sabbath day.
They say prayers
before their meal.

These people live on a kibbutz.
They eat their meals together.
The kibbutz has farms and factories.
Everybody shares the work.

2

The children live and play together.
The babies have beds in a nursery.
A nurse looks after them.

3

Oranges are grown in Israel.
They are sent all over the world.
The oranges are packed in boxes
in a packing house.

4

diamonds

scales

These men are sorting diamonds.
The diamonds will be cut and polished,
then they will be weighed.

Many trees are being planted in Israel.
They are planted
on the edge of the desert.
6

Here is a town in the Negev desert.
The desert has very little water.
Water is brought by pipeline
to the towns.

mule

camel

rugs

Beersheba market is in the desert.
The Bedouins sell animals and goods.
8

Here is a market in Jerusalem.
Jewish food is sold in the market.

This Jewish boy is thirteen.
His father brings him to the synagogue
to say special prayers.
Then he has a party.
10

In the Spring everyone goes
to the Purim festival.
They watch the parade.

Here are some Israeli dancers.
They do a folk dance.
Tourists come to watch them.
12

candlestick

falafel

These tourists are buying presents.
Many tourists buy candlesticks.
A little boy is buying falafel to eat.
Falafel is made of chick peas.

glass

The Red Sea is very warm.
There are strange plants and fish in it.
You can see them
through the glass bottom of the boat.
14

The Dead Sea is very salty.
It is easy to float on it.

Dead
Sea
scrolls

Scrolls were found in caves
near the Dead Sea.
The scrolls told old versions of stories
from the Bible.

This zoo is in Jerusalem.
All the animals in the zoo
are in the Bible.

Jerusalem is a holy city.
It has synagogues,
churches and mosques.
You can see some of them on the map.

18

Wailing Wall

archaeological dig

The Wailing Wall is in Jerusalem.
Everyone comes to look at the wall.
Archaeologists dig there to find
old treasures.

19

Israel long ago

The Bible tells the story
of Israel long ago.
Moses came to Israel with the Jews.
God gave him the Ten Commandments.
20

Jesus was born in a manger
in Bethlehem.
Bethlehem was in the Land of Israel.

The Romans attacked Israel.
They burned the temple.
They made the Jews leave Israel.

22

Some years ago many Jews
went back to Israel.
They were very happy.
They danced in the streets.

paper

string

paints

See if you can make a mask,
like the ones at the Purim festival.
Use string to hold it in place.

24

Starter's **Hebrew** words

Israel	is	ישראל
kibbutz	is	קבוע
diamond	is	יהלם
desert	is	מדבר
synagogue	is	ביח־הכנסת
candlestick	is	פמוט
camel	is	גמל
Dead Sea scrolls	is	מפלות ים המלת
mosque	is	מסגר

People in Israel use the Hebrew alphabet.
Here are some Hebrew words.
They read these words from right to left.

Index